Success with
Scented Plants

D0994033

HELGA AND DIETER MITTMANN

Editor
JOANNA CHISHOLM

MEREHURST

Introduction

A symphony of scents

The spicy scent of herbs, a delicate whiff of roses, the exotic smell of frangipani and the heady perfume of jasmine are just some of the fragrances that the plant kingdom holds in store for you. Why not create your own scented paradise? Large container-plant experts Helga and Dieter Mittmann offer a host of ideas and introduce you to some of the most beautiful species that can be cultivated in large containers. The profusely illustrated section on plant portraits describes where to position your plants and how to care for them.

A separate chapter tells you all about designing with scented plants. Ranging from Mediterranean plants right through to exotic ones, you will learn about some interesting combinations of scented plants and suitable accompaniments. The Care & maintenance section uses clear illustrations to demonstrate the most important rules about watering and overwintering plants.

In addition, there are also some invaluable tips on the use of scented plants – whether as a potpourri or as a delicate ingredient in a drink.

Assisted by this book you will gain considerable pleasure and enjoyment with these wonderful plant scents.

Contents

Many scented plants flourish in the Mediterranean climate.

Scented violet.

Wattakaka (Dregea).

The authors
Helga and Dieter Mittmann own a specialist nursery for large container plants in Salzbergen. They also run a mail order business for young container plants, especially scented ones, and this book is based on their knowledge gained over many years of practical experience.

The photographers
Jürgen Stork specializes in plant photography and has worked for newspapers and periodicals for many years. He has provided photographs for several other titles in the *Success with* series. Further photos are by other well-known plant photographers (see Acknowledgements, p. 61).

The illustrator
Gyorgy Jankovics is a trained graphic design artist who studied at art academies in Budapest and Hamburg. He has provided plant and animal illustrations for a number of reputable publishing houses, and has also produced illustrations for many other titles in the *Success with* series

Important: Please read the Authors' notes on p. 61 so that your enjoyment of scented plants may not be spoiled.

The wonderful world of scents

Scents and odours can stimulate or relax, as well as have a positive effect on the course of some illnesses or possibly conjure up old memories. Many of the most enchanting aromas are derived from the plant kingdom. The next few pages will tell you some fascinating facts about the history, botany and uses of scented plants.

Top: Carnations are just as attractive in a pot as in a flower arrangement.
Left: An exotic corner created by placing together scented plants like oleander and a lemon tree with accompanying plants like Bougainvillea and pomegranate.

The wonderful world of scents

A short history of scented plants

Most people have at one time or the other talked enthusiastically about the marvellous scent of a rose, the heady perfume of jasmine or the stimulating aromas of many herbs. Plants that exude pleasant aromas are classified as scented.

From time immemorial, man has surrounded himself with pleasant odours, which can have a relaxing, calming, stimulating or even healing effect on the body. Because of their mystical and healing effects, the possession and use of scented substances – oils, resins, flowers and leaves – was in the past restricted to priests, medical experts and rulers. Many historians of antiquity reported on the healing and stimulating properties of herbs, roots and flowering plants that were prized and utilized in Asia, Egypt and the Roman Empire. Over the centuries, explorers, conquerors, monks and later merchants introduced many scented plants into the rest of Europe. Initially, the rarer and therefore most expensive and precious scented plants and spices from the temple gardens of Asia and South America were grown only in monastery and abbey gardens and in the orangeries of the ruling houses of Europe. The common people were only familiar with and able to make use of their indigenous scented plants.

Since the Industrial Revolution, large-scale, commercial cultivation of plants and cheaper and better production techniques, using machines to extract scents and oils, have resulted in larger numbers of people gaining access to more exotic scented substances. Traditional uses for scented and aromatic plants can be traced from old plant names and religious rites of the different peoples of Asia and the South Seas. Both the sacrifice of the scented temple flower – the frangipani (*Plumeria*) – and the wearing of flower garlands are still integral parts of religious ceremonies. Aromatherapy, an ancient therapy recently rediscovered, harkens back to the old knowledge about the healing and helpful effects of different scented plants.

Processing plant scents

In the past, essential oils could only be extracted labour-intensively through cold pressing and in very small quantities. While Cleopatra required thousands of flowers or petals for a scented bath, nowadays just a few drops of usually synthetically produced essential oils will be sufficient. Most scented oils would be far too expensive for the average consumer if they were produced only from natural ingredients, because huge quantities of petals are still required for minute quantities of natural oils.

Most people, when sniffing a delicious perfume, are reminded of the deep violet colour of lavender flowers and of the many colours of roses in the fields of Provence. Over the centuries the mixing of perfumes has developed into a major industry there and is a main source of income for the capital, Grasse. The so-called "noses" – the people who create the new perfumes – are highly paid and well-respected specialists.

Even if it is not feasible to manufacture your own essential oils, because the flowers on your balcony or patio could not provide sufficient petals, there are still many uses to which you can put your scented plants (see Flower potpourris, p. 13, Scented cushions and sachets, p.13, Scented flowers in the kitchen, p.13).

The following pages will show you what an abundance of natural scents there are.

Many scented Pelargonium also have attractive flowers.

The wonderful world of scents

Why plants are fragrant

A plant's scent is first and foremost intended to be a lure for insects. These are necessary for the reproduction of certain plant species as they are indispensible for pollination. When insects feed on nectar, oils or resins, pollen adheres to their bodies and so they carry the pollen across to other flowers and complete the pollination process. Particularly in tropical rainforests, plants that do not bear colourful flowers will instead attract pollinating insects with a vast variety of scents. Some odours are very strong, and they range from alluringly sweet right through to foul-smelling stenches – all measured, of course, by our human sense of smell. "Negative" scents are mainly produced by plants for their own defence against predators. A few plants however are pollinated by flies that live on decaying matter, and these plants produce a fly-enticing odour that we would find offensive; various members of the Araceae family belong to this plant group.

How plants produce their scent

Flowers, leaves, bark, fruit and roots can all serve as scent carriers. In some species several parts of the plant contain scented substances – some plants even producing different aromas in different parts. Among these scented substances are essential oils, which are manufactured by the plant using a complicated chemical process.

Depending on the way the perfume is released, a distinction is made between leaf- and flower-scented plants. In leaf- or "contact"-scented plants, the scent carriers are arranged on the leaves and will not release their scented substances until they are touched (contact) or rubbed. When rubbing a leaf, for example, the fine film of skin of the scent gland pops and the special aroma becomes noticeable. Among leaf-scented plants are all herbs like basil (*Ocimum basilicum*), lavender (*Lavandula*) and mint (*Mentha*). Scented *Pelargonium* with their numerous aromas also belong among this group. Leaf-scented plants should be placed where they are often touched or brushed or where they can be reached quite easily.

Plants with fragrant flowers only release their scent through these blooms, and this is released without any contact – as with roses (*Rosa*) or jasmine (*Jasminum*).

When do plants release their scent?

Not all plants release their scent by day. Those that do require considerable light and warmth to produce scented substances and to lure insects that are active in the daytime. Most scented plants belong in this group.

Nocturnal- or evening-scented plants are dependent for their pollination on insects that are active at night so they do not begin to release their scent until early evening or nighttime. Their scent is usually sweet and heavy. Typical nighttime-scented plants are angels' trumpets (*Brugmansia*, formerly *Datura*), dame's violet (*Hesperis matronalis*), perennial phlox (*Phlox paniculata*), evening primrose (*Oenothera*), tobacco plant (*Nicotiana alata*) and the unusual marvel of Peru (*Mirabilis jalapa*). Evening-scented plants should be planted near places where you often like to sit later on in the day.

Recognizing scents

As well as classifying scents into four groups (see Plant scent categories, p. 11), any further description of a scent is based on an individual's purely personal experience of each fragrance.

Colourful, scented plants invite you to relax on this patio.

Scent descriptions in books or catalogues should, therefore, always be viewed as subjective, as an odour that may seem very pleasant to one nose may be obtrusive or positively repellent to another.

Often the mere mention of a certain scent will be enough to trigger treasured childhood memories, for example the scent of grandmother's garden pinks so that one can almost smell them. If we come across descriptions of scents that are alien to us, our imagination cannot cope and quite simply goes on strike. Memory and imagination are strongly stimulated by plants like mint or scented *Pelargonium* that can, for example, make their own species-typical scent dominate other strong odours such as apples or lemons. With the many new hybrids being created, it is difficult to pick up the different scents; as their numbers are steadily increasing, the differences are often just nuances. In such cases, scent descriptions can be confusing and the plant lover can really only depend on his/her own nose.

The wonderful world of scents

How to obtain scented plants

There are many different ways to acquire scented plants:
● You can ask friends and relatives, in which case you can check on the exact scent nuance yourself.
● Often collectors will offer plants for swapping or sale in specialist periodicals. They may have collections of many well-known and rarer species.
● Nurseries and garden centres will carry only a small standard range as a rule.
● Specialist nurseries may offer an extensive scented-plant range. You will have to rely on the description of the scents, but you will be able to acquire the plants quickly by mail order. Some nurseries also carry indigenous wild plants among which there are many species with interesting fragrances.
Our tip: The best plan is to rely on your own sense of smell.

Suitable plant species

The range of scented plants that are suitable for a balcony or patio is colourful and rich in aromas, from annuals, herbaceous plants and bulbs through small garden bushes and trees to exotic, large container plants. Low-growing, scented annuals can be grown in a single dish or as a decorative underplanting with small trees. Scented herbaceous plants, lilies or roses can be kept in pots for a while – as long as the container, the position and the care of the plant keep the plant happy (see pp.18–35). Provided you consider the requirements of each individual plant, you can create the right circumstances for enjoying your plants for many years.

The right position

Most scented plants come from sunny regions like the Mediterranean area or from the relevant climatic zone in Asia, South Africa or Australia. This means they require a bright or even brightly sunlit

This strawberry pot filled with thyme exuded a memorable scent.

position. The scent also develops better in sun. In particular evening- and night-scented plants usually prefer a position in front of a wall that absorbs heat; there they are able to reveal their scent particularly well.

All scented plants should be well protected from the wind so that their aroma cannot disperse too quickly.

Care and maintenance in winter depends on the type of plant:

● Container plants should be stored in a frost-free, usually fairly bright place.

● Hardy plants can be left on a balcony or patio but will need to be protected against very cold weather (see Overwintering, p. 54).

Controlling the amount of scent

Scented plants on a balcony or patio can create a welcome feast for the senses. Too large a collection of different scents, however, can result in exactly the opposite effect – a veritable scent orgy that may be oppressive and even a nuisance. In order to experience and enjoy the positive effect of the scents, only a few, really enchanting fragrances should be chosen and these should be carefully positioned.

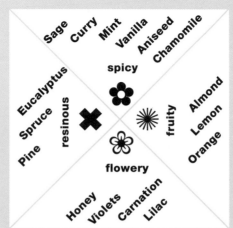

The scent square (left) has been divided up according to the four main categories of scents; within each group you will find certain "leader" scents that are also mentioned in the plant portraits (see pp. 18–33) and in the table (see pp. 34–5).

Plant scent categories

Botanists and psychologists have been attempting to catalogue plant scents since about 1750, and they have grouped certain aromatic characteristics into four main categories: fruity, spicy, flowery and resinous.

When describing scents, in addition to that of smell the sense of taste also plays an important part.

Scents that involved both our senses of taste and smell are easy to categorize:

● Fruity scents like apple, pineapple, peach or strawberry.

● Spicy or aromatic scents like lavender, bay laurel, thyme and vanilla.

The other two categories, on the other hand, are pure scents:

● Flowery scents like rose, carnation and jasmine.

● Resinous scents like spruce, pine and incense. These two large groups have been subdivided again for further identification into flowery, fruity, herby/spicy and resinous types.

Also the different individual plants can be distinguished by the strength of their aroma.

This very clear and easy-to-follow means of identification has not been successfully adopted on a scientific level.

The wonderful world of scents

A potpourris of dried petals and a bunch of lavender will introduce wonderful scents into the home.

Preserving flower scents

Flowers and leaves can be dried in various ways.
To air dry flowers you will need a dry, warm place with sufficient air flow. Flowers will fade if subjected to direct sunlight.

Bunches or single flowers can be hung upside down by their stalks, but first remove the leaves. Bind the bunches tightly (with a rubber band) but do not make them too thick. Attach single flowers to some string or a piece of fine wire.

Single flowers and leaves can be laid out. In order to ensure a good flow of air on all sides, the plants should be laid out singly and be well spaced. A frame with fine-gauge wire or a tray lined with paper towel is suitable as a surface to dry flowers on.

Small quantities can also be dried quickly in an oven (set at 90°C/195°F). Check frequently to prevent the plants from burning.

Preserving single flowers and leaves in silicon gel is also suitable; the colours of the flowers will be particularly well preserved in this way. Silicon gel, which can be obtained at a chemist, can be reused again and again – providing it is dried out in an oven after use and is then stored in an airtight container. Place a 1–2 cm ($^1/_2$–$^3/_4$ in) thick layer of gel in a small cardboard box and lay the flowers on top. Completely cover the flowers with the gel. After a few days, the blue gel will have turned white and can then be carefully removed from the dried flowers.

Flower potpourris

Dried flower petals mixed together and placed in a flat dish surrounded by attractive accessories can be used for months as a scented potpourri. For a spicy potpourri, mix together different aromatic herbs. Potpourris look particularly decorative in attractive ceramic dishes.
Our tip: Fresh scented flowers keep well in a flat glass bowl filled with water. They will last for several days.
Aromatic boxes can be filled with dried flowers and positioned so that you catch their scent as you pass by.
Freshening up potpourris: A few drops of essential oil added to a potpourri when the scent is fading will revive its

fragrance. Sprinkle the drops directly onto the material. The scent will last longer and remain stronger if the potpourri is stored with the essential oil in a closed jar for several days.

Scented cushions and sachets

Scented or herby cushions are intended to relax the user and encourage sleep. You will need a small cushion measuring about 30 x 30 cm (12 x 12 in). Use a piece of pure sheep's wool as an insert. Chamomile, lavender, thyme and rosemary are suitable as a filling. Fill the cushion with *Eucalyptus*, chamomile or mint for cold-sufferers. A few drops of essential oils will revive the scent.
Scented sachets: Small sachets made of decorative material can be filled with dried flower potpourri (rose or lavender) or dried herbs. Close them with a tight tie and hang them up on a piece of string. When the initial aroma has dispersed, again the scent can be refreshed quite easily with essential oil.
Our tip: Sachets filled with lavender are a traditional home remedy to deter moths. Place them in an airing cupboard, wardrobe or drawer.

Scented flowers in the kitchen

Scented flowers and leaves can be used to flavour food and drinks. We recommend using fresh flower petals or herbs in the following recipes.
Rose petal punch: 200 g (7 oz) scented rose petals, 100 g (3$^1/_2$ oz) wild rose flowers, 150 g (5 oz) caster sugar, 100 ml (3$^1/_2$ fl oz) Grand Marnier, 1 litre (1$^3/_4$ pt) dry white wine, and 700 ml (26 fl oz) dry sparkling wine. Wash the flower petals under cold running water and place in large punchbowl, sprinkle sugar on top and dribble the Grand Marnier over the petals. Cover and allow to soak for 1 hour in the fridge. Then pour in the cooled wine and allow to chill for a further 1$^1/_2$ hours. Separate the liquid from the petals and pour in the cooled sparkling wine just before serving; decorate with a few fresh rose petals.
Rose petal tea: One handful scented rose petals in $^3/_4$ litre (27 fl oz) hot water. Allow to steep for 10 minutes.
Herb oils: Place some herbs whose taste you particularly like in a bottle and fill up with a neutral-tasting oil like sunflower oil. Allow to stand in a sunny position for several weeks until the oil has absorbed the aromatic substances of the herbs.

Scented plant portraits

There is a whole host of scented plants to choose from: those from warm regions, which have to be overwintered inside, as well as native plants, which can remain outside in winter. The following plant portraits should make your selection easier.

Top: Many insects like this butterfly are attracted by scented plants.
Left: Oleander, a classic large-container plant, comes in many colours – from white to pink and apricot and salmon to red.

Scented flower portraits

Botanical names

For all plants we have given both the common (English) name and the botanical (Latin) name. The latter clearly defines an individual plant so there can be no confusion when you ask for a particular plant at a garden centre or nursery. The botanical name generally comprises:

● The genus name, for example *Citrus*.
● The species name, for example *limon*.

Citrus limon is therefore the correct botanical name for the lemon tree.

How the plant portraits are arranged

The plant portraits are divided into two groups.

Container plants that are derived from southern, warmer regions, mainly from the Mediterranean area, and which have to be brought inside in winter. There they will usually need a cool place during this rest period, when they will require only little water and no fertilizer. You will find information on their individual winter requirements within the plant portraits.

Hardy plants are normally garden plants (annuals, herbaceous plants, shrubs and trees) that can also be grown in containers or boxes. Although they can remain outside in winter, they may require occasional protection. You will find relevant notes within each plant portrait (see also Overwintering, p. 54). Generally garden plants that are grown in a container will require a little more care than those grown in beds or borders. The information on watering and fertilizing in each plant portrait is only a guide. The plants have been placed alphabetically according to the botanical name within the two groups, with the exception of the herbs, which have been placed together at the end of the Hardy plants.

Explanation of key words

Some basic information is given at the start of each portrait, using symbols. A general introduction to the plant is then succeeded by a more detailed description of the following aspects of the plant.

Scent describes the main or "leader" scent and the sub-scent and will mention if the plant is night-scented.

Care includes the main information on fertilizing and pruning as well as any special care requirements of individual plant species.

Overwintering for container plants explains what position they should be grown in and what care that plant requires.

Pests & diseases mentions the most prevalent pests and diseases.

Note discusses any remarkable features of the plant.

Species mentions the most beautiful and easy-to-care species of a genus.

Our tip gives advice from the years of experience gained by both authors.

Caution refers not only to toxic plants but also to those that irritate skin or trigger an allergy.

Explanation of symbols

 scented flowers

 scented leaves

 flowering time (see p. 61)

 needs full sun

 needs light

 needs semi-shade

 needs shade

 water copiously

 water moderately

 water sparingly

 toxic

Heliotrope and lilies enchant with their scent and colour.

Large container plants

Large container plants can bring a touch of southern flair to more northern countries – as well as being very attractive and scented. With good care and appropriate overwintering techniques, many of these plants will give you much pleasure for many a long year.

Acacia is often erroneously called mimosa.

Large container plants have been very popular for a long time, even in countries of northern latitudes. The classic large container plants like citrus fruit trees and oleander (*Nerium oleander*) with their wonderful scents gave pleasure to many a Baroque nobleman. Attached to many castles and stately houses were "orangeries", in which large container plants were overwintered. Before purchasing a large container plant, you need to consider whether you will be able to offer it a suitable place for the winter period. As these plants usually originate from the Mediterranean area or even warmer climates,

they will be frost tender or half hardy, so during the winter months, they will require mostly coolish temperatures, of 8–12°C (46–54°F). This is often difficult to achieve in a centrally heated home. A warm conservatory is, of course, ideal for overwintering where you will also have the added pleasure of experiencing winter-flowering plants such as Mexican orange blossom (*Choisya ternata*), *Eriobotrya* or *Solandra*.

You must be careful if you store scented plants in an unventilated room where you spend a lot of time, because strong scents may provoke headaches.

Acacia
acacia, wattle

Vigorous, evergreen trees with small globular flower clusters.

Scent: Flowery: strong, smell of honey.
Care: Fertilize every 2 weeks. Does not like chalk (alkaline soil).
Overwintering: Bright position, 5–12°C (41–54°F), water less after flowering.
Pests & diseases:

Spider mites, mealy bugs.
Our tip: *A. retinodes* flowers all year round.
Caution: Sharp thorns can cause injury.

Acacia flowers.

Even the leaves of the silk tree are decorative.

Angels' trumpet reveals its magic scent at night.

Albizia jullbrissin silk tree

 MS–EA

Deciduous tree or small bush with decorative, feathery leaves that fold up at night "to sleep". The flowers with their long, reddish pink filaments are reminiscent of small powder puffs.
Scent: Flowery, slightly sweet.
Care: Fertilize weekly during the summer. This plant requires well-drained potting compost. Cut back late in winter. Relatively easy to care for, very robust.
Overwintering: Cool (also dark) at 0–8°C (32–46°F), keep dry.
Pests & diseases: Mealy bugs; fungal infestation of the roots possible if it is kept too wet.

Brugmansia (formerly *Datura*) angels' trumpets

 MS–LA

Deciduous, fast-growing plants with large leaves and pendulous trumpets, up to 30 cm (12 in) long, in shades of white, pink, yellow, apricot; with single or double flowers.
Scent: Flowery: intense, heady perfume. Night scented.
Care: Weekly fertilizing with granules. Remove old flowers. When storing for the winter, prune back by about a third.
Overwintering: Does not like frost. Keep at 5°C (41°F), in bright or dark conditions, water sparingly.
Pests & diseases: Vine weevils, red spider mites, mealy bugs.
Caution: Toxic. The strong scent may cause headaches.

Scented plant portraits

Citrus
citrus

  ESP–LW

This genus includes a wide range of evergreen fruit-bearing trees with shiny leaves and white, pleasantly scented flowers. Flowers and fruits will appear simultaneously on partially spiny branches. On the new shoots, the flowers tend to appear before the leaves.

Scent: Fruity: strong sweet, orangy scent.

Care: Only use water that is lime-free; during the summer, water profusely every 2–3 days. Avoid waterlogging. Fertilize every 2 weeks. Fertilizer containing iron will help with chlorosis.

Overwintering: Bright and definitely cool, at 5–12° C (41–54°F), and keep almost completely dry during this time.

Pests & diseases: Mealy bugs, scale insects, spider mites, chlorosis (often triggered by water containing too much lime). Loss of leaves

All citrus plants bear flowers at the same time as fruit.

due to draughts.

Species: *C. limon* (lemon) grows profusely; *C. reticulata* (mandarin) and *C.* x *nobilis* (Florida orange) tend to remain small; *C. aurantium* (Seville orange) has an attractive growing shape.

Note: *Citrus* requires protection from wind and continuous rainfall.

Our tip: Choose only citrus plants that have been grown from cuttings; plants grown from seed will hardly flower at all.

Caution: The thorns of some species can cause injury.

Mandarins.

Heliotrope exudes a strong scent of vanilla.

All jasmine species have an intense scent.

Heliotropium arborescens cherry pie, heliotrope

 ES–MA

Evergreen semi-bush with rough, olive-green leaves. *H. arborescens* tends to grow sideways and spread out. Its flower umbels comprise numerous small dark violet flowers.

Scent: Flowery: very intense scent of vanilla.

Care: On hot days, water more than usual; fertilize weekly. The plant should never be allowed to dry out. Remove faded flowers regularly.

Overwintering: Bright, around 10°C (50°F), keep almost dry.

Pests & diseases: Whitefly, spider mites.

Note: Heliotropes require a position sheltered from the wind.

Our tip: Depending on the shape of growth, heliotrope is also suitable for boxes and hanging baskets. It combines well with other summer-flowering plants.

Caution: Toxic. The intense scent in close proximity or in unventilated rooms may cause headaches.

Jasminum jasmine

 LSP–LS 🔆 💧

Evergreen, usually vigorous climbing plants of many species with perfumed, white or yellow clusters of flowers.

Scent: Flowery: intense perfume of jasmine.

Care: Fertilize every 2 weeks. Prune vigorously after flowering.

Overwintering: Bright, at 5–8°C (41–46°F); water sparingly.

Pests & diseases: Aphids, spider mites.

Species: *J. angulare* with white flowers and a fainter scent; *J. officinale* (common jasmine) with white flowers and intense perfume; *J. humile* 'Revolutum' with yellow flowers and a fainter scent; *J. laurifolium* f. *nitidum* with white flowers and an intense perfume.

Caution: The intensely strong scent may cause headaches.

Scented plant portraits

The leaves and flowers of bay laurel are fragrant.

Chilean jasmine has a strong but toxic scent.

Laurus nobilis
bay laurel

Evergreen, slow-growing bush or tree with matt to shiny, spicy-smelling leaves. Scented, whitish-yellow flowers in the spring. Grown for its decorative effect and its scented foliage. The leaves can be used in cooking.

Scent: Flowery/spicy: the flowers have a slight scent of honey and the leaves smell spicy.

Care: Very robust and easy to care for. Fertilize every 2 weeks in the summer. Will tolerate a few degrees of frost.

Overwintering: Frost-free but cool; also dark. Water sparingly.

Pests & diseases: Mealy bugs, scale insects; aphids on new shoots.

Note: Bay laurel will flourish in a sunny position as well as in shade.

Our tip: Bay laurel is very effective pruned as a tall tree or into a pyramid shape.

Mandevilla laxa
Chilean jasmine

This deciduous plant bears thin, delicate shoots with oval- to lance-shaped leaves that turn a reddish colour in cool weather. It bears large, strongly scented, funnel-shaped, white flowers. Chilean jasmine tends to become bare from the bottom upwards.

Scent: Flowery: sweetish; similar to hyacinth.

Care: Plant in rich potting compost, fertilize every 2 weeks. Bare patches can be covered up quite easily if the new, longer shoots are allowed to hang over them. Tolerates a vigorous prune in autumn.

Overwintering: Cool at 2–5°C (36–41°F), bright or dark. Keep almost dry.

Pests & diseases: Aphids, spider mites.

Caution: All parts of the plant are toxic. The milky juice that emerges when cutting back the plant can irritate skin or cause allergic reactions.

Only older evergreen magnolias bear their splendid flowers.

Mirabilis jalapa
marvel of Peru

 MS–EA

Bushy shrub with vigorous tuberous roots. The flowers are yellow, white, pink or even multi-coloured. A plant can bear flowers of different colours, hence its name.

Scent: Fruity: a strong scent, reminiscent of oranges. Night-scented.

Care: Fertilize weekly during the summer. The tubers can be allowed to shoot from early spring onwards in a warm, bright position. This plant is also easy to grow from seed.

Overwintering: Frost-free and dry, so it will produce more and more flowers from year to year.

Pests & diseases: Aphids.

Our tip: Position this plant close to a sitting area as it develops a wonderfully seductive scent in the evening.

Magnolia
grandiflora
bull bay

Evergreen plant with large, creamy-white flowers that tend to develop only on older plants.

Scent: Flowery: aromatic sweet

Care: Fertilize generously in summer. Cut back in late summer. Susceptible to sunburn.

Overwintering: Light, at 0–8°C (32–46°F); keep fairly moist.

Pests & diseases: Aphids.

Marvel of Peru.

Scented plant portraits

Nerium oleander ☠
Oleander

Oleander is the classic large container plant *per se*, and is also very robust. This evergreen tree or bush with long, leathery leaves bears white, pink, red, apricot, salmon or yellow flowers – single or double. Double flowers have a stronger scent but, due to their weight, may be more susceptible to rain damage. Oleander will flower particularly abundantly in warm, sunny years; in rainy, cool summers the flowers will be sparse.
Scent: Flowery, intensely sweet smell.
Care: Grow in humus-rich, chalky soil or potting compost; also tolerates hard water. Requires generous fertilizer in summer. Protect flowers from heavy or continuous rain, otherwise they will become brown and unsightly. Vigorous pruning is recommended when the plant begins to look bare. Oleander

The double flowers of some oleander species smell stronger.

tolerates a light frost.
Overwintering: At 0–8°C (32–46°F), light or dark, water sparingly.
Pests & diseases: Scale insects, mealy bugs, spider mites, oleander tumours.
Our tip: Oleander kept in a warm conservatory may even produce flowers all year round.
Caution: All parts of oleander are highly toxic. After repotting or cutting back, always wash hands thoroughly. The intense scent may cause headaches in close proximity or in unventilated rooms.

Single oleander flower.

Pittosporum has shiny leaves and white flowers.

Frangipani flowers produce a heady scent.

Pittosporum tobira Japanese mock orange

  LW–LSP

Decorative, evergreen bush with shiny, leathery, green or variegated leaves, which are also very attractive. The scented, creamy-white flowers develop in short umbels. Japanese mock orange takes its name from the sticky fleshed fruits that surround the seeds.
Scent: Flowery: sweetish, smells slightly of honey.
Care: Humus-rich soil or potting compost, fertilize well in summer. Japanese mock orange is very robust and easy to care for.
Overwintering: Bright and cool at 0–8°C (32–46°F), water sparingly.
Pests & diseases: Aphids on new shoots.
Further species: P. tobira 'Nanum' is smaller and more compact.
Note: Will still flourish fairly well even in semi-shade.
Our tip: Japanese mock orange is easy to prune into a rounded shape at any time of year.

Plumeria frangipani, pagoda tree

  ES–EA

Deciduous or semi-evergreen trees or bushes with long, oval leaves that grow only on the ends of the succulent shoots. The large, scented, wax-like flowers develop in false umbels at the shoot tips.
Scent: Flowery: strong sweet scent.
Care: Water with lime-free water and fertilize sparingly. Use good-quality, well-drained compost to prevent waterlogging.
Overwintering: Bright and warm at 12–20°C (54–68°F), keep almost dry.
Pests & diseases: Spider mites, mealy bugs.
Species: P. alba (West Indian jasmine) bears white flowers with yellow centres; P. rubra (common frangipani) has white, yellow, red, pink or purple flowers.
Our tip: This plant is not quite so easy to care for and is recommended only for experienced gardeners.
Caution: The milky sap on this plant may cause skin irritation or allergies.

Hardy plants

Even plant lovers who have no proper facilities for overwintering large container plants can still grow attractive scented flowers. A whole range of garden plants, such as annuals, herbaceous plants, shrubs and small trees, can be grown in small pots and containers and overwintered on balconies or patios.

Plants in pots, tubs, windowboxes or hanging baskets are considerably more sensitive than plants cultivated in the open garden and so need greater care. Many plants that are hardy in borders and beds also require winter protection if grown on a balcony or patio (see Overwintering, p. 54).

Chocolate vine (Akebia) is a vigorous climber.

Akebia quinata chocolate vine

 MSP–LSP

This vigorous climber will retain its foliage in mild regions. The purple-violet flowers hang in clusters and may occasionally suffer damage from late frosts.
Scent: Fruity: a strong scent of orange and vanilla.
Care: Humus-rich, porous soil or potting compost, fertilizer every 2 weeks and a good climbing aid will encourage chocolate vine to grow very fast. The new shoots will often entwine. You can prevent this by training all the shoots. A vigorous prune after flowering will prevent the plant becoming leggy or growing too much.
Pests & diseases: None.
Note: Will also flourish in sunny and shady positions.

Lily-of-the-valley is a scented herald of spring.

Dame's violet has beautiful night-scented blooms.

Convallaria majalis lily-of-the-valley

One of the first harbingers of spring, lily-of-the-valley bears delicate, white, little bell flowers arranged in a row on stalks.
Scent: Flowery: strong characteristic scent of lily-of-the-valley.
Care: Humus-rich soil or potting compost; fertilize sparingly every 2 weeks. Lily-of-the-valley will also flourish in a bright position.
Pests & diseases: None.
Note: Some species produce pink or double flowers, some varieties also have variegated leaves.
Our tip: We recommend using this plant only in a single group or for underplanting, for example with angels' trumpets, as it spreads vigorously.
Caution: Toxic in all parts, especially the red berries.

Hesperis matronalis dame's violet, sweet rocket

This night-scented plant with its oval leaves and long, violet or white spikes has very upright growth. Dame's violet can attain heights of about 50–70 cm (20–28 in).
Scent: Fruity: delicate, slightly sweet scent of carnations and oranges. Night-scented.
Care: Deadhead regularly.
Pests & diseases: None.
Note: Dame's violet will flourish even in semi-shade.
Our tip: Choose a tall pot for this plant as it develops long roots; the pot should also stand very firmly as the plant can overbalance easily because of its height.

27

Scented plant portraits

Passiflora caerulea
blue passion flower

  ESP–LW ○

This fast-growing climbing plant bears 7 cm (3 in) wide, white and blue flowers. It particularly likes a position in front of a warm, sunny wall and is only slightly hardy.
Scent: Flowery: light scent.
Care: Fertilize every 2 weeks. Tolerates pruning well. Cover if overwintered outside (see Overwintering, p. 54). Prefers a frost-free environment, at 5–8°C (41–46°F); then water sparingly.
Pests & diseases: Spider mites.
Our tip: P. x belotii 'Impératrice Eugénie' with its large, scented, lilac-coloured

Delightfully fragrant honeysuckle makes an excellent visual screen.

flowers is a particularly beautiful passion flower.

Passiflora x belotii 'Impératrice Eugénie'

Lonicera
honeysuckle

Usually deciduous climbers with woody shoots and rolled-up, pipe-like flowers. Carries attractive berries in the autumn.
Scent: Flowery: sweet. Night-scented.
Care: Fertilize every 14 days, cut back by about a third every autumn.
Pests & diseases: Aphids.

Species:
L. caprifolium (Italian honeysuckle) with orange-yellow flowers and L. periclymenum 'Graham Thomas' with white flowers are very strongly scented. L. brownii 'Dropmore Scarlet' with orange-red flowers and L. japonica 'Halliana' with white flowers smell less strong.
Caution: All honeysuckles are toxic.

Cotton lavender looks good alone or mixed.

Butterflies are attracted to Viburnum's scent.

Santolina cotton lavender

 MS–LS

Evergreen, rounded semi-bushes with fine, aromatic foliage and small, button-like, yellow flowers. The plant grows 20–40 cm (8–16 in) high.
Scent: Spicy: a pleasant scent of chamomile and cypress.
Care: Fertilize sparingly. Cotton lavender requires poor soil or compost. If it becomes increasingly leggy, pruning it into shape should help. In regions with cold winter conditions, cover it up (see Overwintering, p. 54).
Pests & diseases: None.
Our tip: Cotton lavender is very suitable for combining with roses but not in the same container. It also makes an attractive accompaniment to Mediterranean plants.

Viburnum viburnum

 MSP–LSP

Deciduous bushes with large, pink or white flower umbels. Carries attractive berries in the autumn.
Scent: Flowery: intense, heavy perfume.
Care: Fertilize every 2 weeks during the summer months; cut back after flowering.
Pests & diseases: Aphids.
Species: V. x *burkwoodii* with pink flowers; V. x *bodnantense* depending on the variety with pink or white-pink flowers; *V. carlesii* with white flowers; and V. x *juddii* with white flowers. These species have a particularly strong scent, although all *Viburnum* species have some scent.
Note: Will also flourish in bright or semi-shady positions.

Scented plant portraits

Herbs – Spicy and decorative

Herbs, being "touchable scents" will make wonderful accessories for an attractive design. Below we introduce you to some herbs.

Ocimum basilicum
basil

MS–LS

This annual herb, depending on the variety, will bear green or reddish leaves with whitish pink flowers.
Scent: Spicy: depending on the species, for example cinnamon or aniseed.
Care: Fertilize every 2 weeks.
Pests & diseases: Aphids.
Note: Basil can be sown in a warm position from early spring onwards. Alternatively, stand bought plants outside after the last frosts.
Our tip: If you wish to dry basil leaves, you should cut off the shoots shortly before the basil comes into bloom.

Mentha
mint

ES–EA

These herbaceous plants have aromatic leaves and white, blue or pink blooms. There are numerous new hybrids with variations on leaves and scents.
Scent: Spicy or fruity, according to the species.
Care: Prune vigorously in late autumn. Divide frequently as mint develops lots of runners, and to prevent it from becoming leggy.
Pests & diseases: None.
Species: M. x piperita with a refreshing scent, M. x p. f. citrata (eau-de-Cologne mint) with an orangy aroma, M. suaveolens (apple mint) with a faint hint of apples. M.s. 'Variegata' (pineapple mint) with a full scent of pineapples.

Rosmarinus officinalis
rosemary

LSP–MS

Decorative, small evergreen bushes with needle-like foliage. The flowers are lilac, pink or white.
Scent: Spicy: very tangy.
Care: Requires very well-drained, loamy-sandy soil or potting compost; dislikes waterlogged soil. Fertilize sparingly. Can be pruned after flowering.
Pests & diseases: None.
Note: Hardy only in mild climate regions.

Salvia
sage

ES–EA

Herbaceous or evergreen perennials or shrubs with numerous leaf and flower shapes.
Scent: Spicy, fruity or resinous, depending on the species.
Care: Fertilize sparingly. Requires soil or potting compost that contains lime. Pruning can be done in spring or autumn. Overwinter in frost-free conditions at 5–8°C (41–46°F).
Pests & diseases: Whitefly, mildew.
Species: S. clevelandii (Jim sage) with blue flowers and a pleasant spicy scent; S. greggii (autumn sage) with pink flowers and a delicate peach scent; S. rutilans (pineapple sage) with red flowers and a fruity scent of pineapple; S. sclarea (clary sage) with pink or blue flowers and a light resinous aroma.

Thymus
Thyme

LSP–MA

Spreading, semi-bushes with white, pink or pale blue flowers. Very popular with bees.
Scent: Spicy or fruity, depending on the species.
Care: Well-drained, alkaline soil or compost. Remove dead flowers and leaves.
Pests & diseases: None.
Species: T. vulgaris (garden thyme) with a spicy-minty aroma; T. x citriodorus (lemon-scented thyme) with a fresh lemony scent.
Note: Thyme is good as underplanting and in hanging baskets.

A corner on a balcony filled with pleasantly scented, decorative herbs.

Rosa 'Charles Austin'.

Roses – Romantic dispensers of scent

The rose is probably everyone's idea of the ultimate source of scent or perfume, although only about a quarter of all rose varieties are scented. The very old roses have particularly strong and enchanting perfumes. Take a look around among the roses of a dedicated gardener or in a gardening catalogue and you will discover many utterly beautiful and wonderfully scented varieties.

Rosa 'Shocking Blue' creates accents with its scent and colour.

Rosa 'Ena Harkness'.

Rosa 'Fantin-Latour'.

Although the rose is considered to be a classic bedding plant, a few species are also eminently suited to growing in pots. Consider the following criteria when making your choices:

● Suitability for cultivation in pots.
● Intensity of scent and colour of flowers.
● Growth habit and height of growth.
● Flowering once or several times.

Roses require a tall pot to grow in. If there is an underplanting of accompanying plants, make sure that the rose is always the main feature or centrepiece.

Caution: *Watch out for the well-known, sharp thorns.*

Rosa 'New Dawn'.

Rosa 'Morning Jewel'.

Scented plant portraits

Scent calendar: Further scented plants and their flowering times

	Botanical name / English name	Leader scent / Scented leaf/flower	Flowering month / Flower colour	Position / Watering	Comments
🌸🌸🌸	*Acidanthera bicolor,* syn. *Gladiolus callianthus* / Night-scented	honey / flower	MS–LS / white	☼ / ✧	Night-scented, bulb/tuber; overwinter inside
🌸🌸	*Alyssum maritimum* / Sweet alyssum	honey / flower	LSP–LS / white, blue	☼ / ✧	Annual, low-growing for flat bowls or underplanting
🌸🌸🌸	*Boronia heterophylla* / Kalgan, Red boronia	honey / flower	MSP–ES / dark pink	☼ / ✧	Evergreen, use soft water (no lime), keep moist; winter: very bright 5–10°C (41–50°F)
🌸🌸🌸	*Cheiranthus cheiri* ☠ / Wallflower	violet / flower	MSP–MS / yellow, orange, red	☼ ✿	Biennial, cut back after flowering; grow outside in winter; very toxic seeds
🌸🌸	*Colletia cruciata* / Colletia	honey / flower	ES–EA / white	☼ / ✧	Leafless, thorny bush, fertilize only every 4 weeks; winter: bright, 5°C (41°F)
🌸🌸	*Dianthus* / Carnation, Pink	carnation / flower	LSP–EA / white, pink, red	☼ / ✧	Evergreen, use low-growing varieties for pots; grow outside in winter
🌸🌸	*Dregea sinensis* / Wattakaka	honey / flower	MSP–MA / white, pink	☼ ◐ / ✦	Deciduous climber, milky sap may cause allergies; winter: light/dark, 0–8°C (32–46°F), dry
🌸🌸	*Exacum affine* / Persian violet	honey / flower	ES–EA / violet	☼ / ✧	May last for several years if overwintered inside, good for bowls or balcony boxes
🌸	*Filipendula* / Filipendula	honey / flower	MS–LS / white	☼ ◐ / ✧	*F. ulmaria* (meadowsweet) particularly suitable
🌸	*Iberis amara* / Candytuft	honey / flower	LSP–LS / white	☼ / ✧	Annual, easy to care for, profusely flowering; good for underplanting and balcony boxes
🌸🌸	*Lathyrus odoratus* / Sweet pea	honey / flower	ES–EA / many colours	☼ / ✦	Climber, low-growing species also for balcony boxes
🌸🌸🌸	*Lilium regale* / Regal lily	honey / flower	MS–LS / white, pink	☼ / ✧	Bulb/tuber; overwinter inside; further species *L. candidum*, *L. speciosum*
🌸	*Melia azedarach* / Bead tree	lilac / flower	MSP–ES / violet	☼ / ✦	Deciduous, attractive berries, decorative growth; winter: bright or dark, c.5°C (41°F)
🌸🌸	*Oenothera odorata* ☠ / Evening primrose	honey / flower	ES–EA / yellow	☼ ◐ / ✧	Biennial or perennial, night-scented, sandy soil/compost, plant in tall pots
🌸🌸🌸	*Ornithogalum thyrsoides* / Star of Bethlehem	honey / flower	ES–MA / white	☼ / ✧	Bulb/tuber, continuous flowering; winter: light, 5–8°C (41–46°F)
🌸🌸🌸	*Petunia x hybrida* ☠ / Petunia	honey / flower	LSP–MA / blue-violet	☼ ◐ / ✦	Annual, only blue or violet varieties, strongly scented
🌸🌸🌸	*Reseda odorata* / Common mignonette	violet / flower	ES–LS / yellowish	☼ / ✧	Annual, the strongly scented flowers are inconspicuous, goes well with roses
🌸🌸	*Syringa microphylla* / Lilac	lilac / flower	ES–LS / pink	☼ ◐ / ✦	Deciduous, 'Superba' suitable for growing in large containers, second flowering LS, hardy
🌸🌸	*Viola odorata* / Sweet violet	violet / flower	ESP–MSP / violet, pink, white	☼ ◐ / ✧	Semi-evergreen, propagate from runners; grow outside in winter

🌸 = few flowers   🌸🌸 = moderately floriferous   🌸🌸🌸 = very floriferous   ✳ = few berries   ✳✳ = moderately berried
✳✳✳ = well berried   ✿ = slightly fragrant   ✿✿ = moderately fragrant   ✿✿✿ = highly fragrant

	Botanical name / English name	Leader scent / Scented leaf/flower	Flowering month / Flower colour	Position / Watering	Comments
•••	*Aloysia triphylla* / Lemon verbena	lemon / leaf	ES–LS / white	☼ / ✦	Deciduous, syn. *Lippia citriodora*, robust; winter: light or dark, *c.*5˚C (41˚F), almost dry
••	*Araujia sericifera* / Cruel plant	almond / flower	ES–LA / white, pink	☼ ◑ / ✦	Evergreen climber, milky sap can lead to skin irritation; winter: bright, *c.*5˚C, almost dry
••	*Caryopteris* x *clandonens.* / Bluebeard	lemon / leaf	LS–MA / violet	☼ / ✧	Deciduous; overwinter inside
••	*Dracocephalum moldavic.* / Dragon's head	lemon / leaf	MS–LS / dark blue	☼ / ✧	Annual, very attractive to bees, prefers chalky soil
•••	*Eucalyptus citriodora* / Lemon–scented gum	lemon / leaf	MA–LSP / creamy-white	☼ / ✦	Evergreen, the lemon scent will drive away flies and mosquitoes; winter: bright, *c.*5˚C (41˚F)
••	*Monarda didyma* / Bergamot	orange / leaf	ES–EA / many colours	☼ / ✧	Deciduous; protect outside in winter; other species have different scent nuances
••	*Osmanthus delavayi* / Osmanthus	orange / flower	MSP–ES / white	☼ ● / ✧	Evergreen, very decorative and robust; grow outside in winter
••	*Schizopetalon walkeri* / Schizopetalon	almond / flower	ES–LS / white	☼ / ✧	Annual, night-scented
•••	*Trachelospermum jasmin.* 💀 / Star jasmine	orange/vanilla / flower	ESP–MA / white, yellow	☼ ◑ / ✦	Evergreen climbier; *T. asiaticum* bears continuous yellow flowers; in winter: bright, 0–8˚C (32–46˚F)
✿✿	*Agastache anisata* / Anise hyssop	aniseed / leaf	ES–MA / blue-violet	☼ / ✧	mint-scented *A. rugosa*, citrus-scented *A. mexicana*; overwinter outside
✿✿	*Anthemis nobilis* / Chamomile	chamomile / flower	ES–LS / white	☼ ◑ / ✦	Very suitable as underplanting, syn. *Chamaemelum nobile*
✿✿	*Berlandiera lyrata* / Berlandiera	chocolate / leaf	LSP–MS / yellow	☼ / ✧	Deciduous; overwinter inside
✿✿	*Clematis armandii* / Clematis	vanilla / flower	LSP–LS / white	☼ ◑ / ✦	Outside with frost protection in winter; other species have other scent varieties
✿✿✿	*Helichrysum serotinum* / Curry plant	curry / leaf	LSP–MS / yellow	☼ / ✧	Evergreen, goes well with lavender and rosemary; hardy in milder regions, needs frost protection
✿✿✿	*Lavandula angustifolia* / Lavender	lavender / flower	ES–EA / lilac, pink	☼ / ✧	Evergreen; needs winter protection outside; loves chalky soil; *L. stoechas* has stronger scent
✿✿	*Matthiola* / Gillyflower, Stock	vanilla/cinnamon / flower	LSP–LS / many colours	☼ / ✧	Annual, sow in pots or buy ready grown plants, night-scented
✿✿	*Perovskia atriplicifolia* / Perovskia	sage / leaf	MS–EA / sky-blue	☼ / ✧	Deciduous, semi-bush, decorative grey foliage; overwinter inside
✿✿	*Prostanthera ovalifolia* / Oval-leaved mint bush	mint / leaf	MSP–ES / lilac, white	☼ ● / ✦	Evergreen, very sensitive to waterlogging; winter: much light, 8–12˚C (46–54˚F), almost dry
✿✿	*Schinus molle* / Pepper tree	pepper / leaf, berries	LSP–MA / yellow-white	☼ / ✦	Semi-evergreen, pendulous branches, decorative red berries; winter: bright, 5–12˚C (41–54˚F)

☼ = sun   ◑= semi–shade   ●= shade   ✦ = water copiously   ✧ = water moderately   💀 = toxic

Scented surroundings

Design your own small scented island on a balcony or patio. Select a few non-scented accompanying plants so that the cloud of scents does not become too overpowering. The following pages depict some attractive combinations for you to copy.

Top: Mandarins will probably grow a little smaller on the patio than in open ground.
Left: Lavender (here French lavender) not only impresses with its flowers but also does a marvellous job at deterring aphids.

Scented surroundings

Introducing an exotic touch

You should observe some basic design rules whether you choose exotic, tender plants or some that are able to spend the winter outside in temperate climates. It is generally a good idea, for example, to select large plants that also have an attractive shape as solitary, accent plants, and use smaller plants to accompany them. Scented plants should always be combined with non–scented ones, so that the different aromas remain pleasant and distinguishable and do not overpower. Introduce suitable pots and other accessories (such as the gourds on the opposite page) to enhance the ambience you are trying to create. The following pages introduce plants grouped according to the country in which they originate, because knowing where a plant comes from will help you reproduce similar conditions in your own garden.

Robust Australasian plants

Many plants from Australasia are very easy to care for.
Scented plants: The aroma on the foliage of the fast-growing *Eucalyptus* is reminiscent of cough lozenges. *E. citriodora*, which smells of lemon, is also interesting. Mint bush (*Prostanthera*), with its white and purple flowers, exudes a rather strong odour of mint. In the spring, wattle flowers (*Acacia*) smell sweet, as do the flowers of *Boronia* and the large-leaved Australian frangipani (*Hymenosporum*).
Accompanying plants: The glowing red tassels of the pokutakawa (*Metrosideros*) and bottlebrush (*Callistemon*) trees and the grey-green foliage of pink Norfolk Island hibiscus (*Lagunaria*) alternate with the delicate flowers and the needle-like foliage of tea tree (*Leptospermum*). Even the name reveals the growth habit of the yellow zigzag bush (*Corokia*), which flowers early in spring. The blue flowers of *Alyogyne* are sensitive to rain.
Accompanying climbing plants: Hardenbergia, Sollya, Kennedia and Clianthus belong among these as does the evergreen *Pandorea* with its gleaming foliage and pink, funnel-shaped flowers.

Sun-loving plants from South Africa

Plants that originate from the Cape region of South Africa generally need considerable amounts of sun, as well as much warmth in winter.
Scented plants: Toxic *Carissa*, fine-leaved silk tree (*Albizia julibrissin*) and scented geraniums (*Pelargonium*) all come from this region.
Accompanying plants: Strong colours are displayed by *Lantana* and seneca (*Polygala*).
The blue splashes of colour provided by African blue lily (*Agapanthus*) and cape leadwort (*Plumbago auriculata*) almost compete with the yellow trumpets of *Tecomaria* and the red pea-blossom flowers of the thorny coral tree (*Erythrina*). Particularly decorative flowers grace bird of paradise (*Strelitzia*) and *Bauhinia*. Anisodonthea and yellow senna (*Cassia*) are reliable, perpetual flowerers.

The wealth of flowers from Central America

A vast number of scented plants with intense, sweet perfumes originate from Central America.
Scented plants: Really sweet odours are exuded by milkweed (*Asclepias*), the fast-growing tree tomato (*Cyphomandra*) and *Araujia*. Not only will the white, goblet-shaped flowers of Chilean jasmine (*Mandevilla laxa*) enchant you but also their wonderful scent.
The bizarre appearance of the thorny *Colletia* will be ideal for

Some interesting gourds here enhance the exotic flair of an eye-catching plant combination.

a background planting. A space in the first row, however, should be given to heliotrope (*Heliotropium arborescens*). Night-scented angels' trumpets (*Brugmansia*) are suitable as an accent plant.
Accompanying plants: Try the unscented species of passion flower (*Passiflora*), *Bougainvillea* and *Abutilon* (hibiscus species).

Plants that are native to China

Because the climate in parts of China is similar to that of the Mediterranean area, many plants that originate from China also flourish in Mediterannean regions.
Scented plants: Lemon and orange (*Citrus*), oleander (*Nerium*) and jasmine

(*Jasminum*) all originate from China. *Trachelospermum* and wattakaka (*Dregea*) are both climbers that smell sweet and will flower until autumn.
Accompanying plants: Bamboo is particularly suitable for conjuring up a Chinese atmosphere as well as for introducing a calming green oasis among a multitide of florid colours.

Scented surroundings

Mediterranean scent impressions

Plenty of sun and attractive flowering plants may form part of your holiday memories. Fortunately, Mediterranean plants and a warm summer evening can be sufficient to recreate that southern ambience even in northern latitudes. Many of the most beautiful Mediterranean plants will grow on balconies and patios, but like their more exotic relatives (see Exotic flair, p. 38) they will require a frost-free environment for the winter (see Overwintering, p. 54).

Perfumed messengers from the Mediterranean

As with all plant designs, plants should be arranged according to their height, with taller plants at the back.
Tall/accent plants: Bay laurel (*Laurus nobilis*) and oleander (*Nerium*) as well as the blue-flowering bead tree (*Melia*) fit well into this group. Pepper tree (*Schinus molle*) with its fine leaves should be placed at the sides of a planting so that its long, overhanging branches can look as effective as possible. In such a position, the intense peppery smell of the leaves and seeds can also be enjoyed. Eye-catching frangipani (*Plumeria*) with its

strong scent deserves a sunny position of honour.
Medium-sized plants: Citrus varieties like lemon and orange with their white, strongly sweet-smelling flowers can be placed in the centre of a planting, beside fragrant *Pittosporum*, which is very robust and has an attractive growth habit and foliage.
Low-growing plants: Rock rose (*Cistus*) and sweet–smelling herbs like lavender (*Lavandula*) and rosemary (*Rosmarinus*) should be planted in the foreground, as should *Perovskia* and cotton lavender (*Santolina*).

Beautiful companion plants

It is almost impossible to think of southern latitudes without palm trees. Species like Canary Island date palm (*Phoenix canariensis*), Chusan palm (*Trachycarpus fortunei*) and dwarf fan palm (*Chamaerops humilis*) are suitable for temperate climates and are relatively easy to look after. Laurustinus (*Viburnum tinus*), common fig (*Ficus carica*), strawberry tree (*Arbutus*), olive (*Olea*) and *Ceratonia* are all typically Mediterranean plants that grow fairly slowly and have interesting foliage – as does mastic tree (*Pistacia lentiscus*).

Among the pomegrante (*Punica*) varieties with their red flowers, the dwarf form *P. granatum nana* is best for our climate. The bracts of the thorny climber *Bougainvillea* glow in various shades of red through to violet. Large-flowered rose of China (*Hibiscus rosa-sinensis*) is equally good looking. Succulent plants like *Aeonium* and *Aloe* are undemanding and provide a rustic touch in weathered pots. Shrubby lilyturf (*Liriope*) with its grass-like foliage provides a last splash of colour in autumn with its violet flower spikes.

Terracotta highlights

Terracotta or clay pots with their many different styles make a great contribution to a Mediterranean atmosphere. The photo on pp. 4–5 gives a good idea of how well typically Mediterranean plants like scented lavender (*Lavandula*) and lemon tree (*Citrus limon*) can be combined with more exotic plants such as pomegrante (*Punica granatum*) and *Bougainvillea*. It is not only terracotta pots that are very decorative; small statues made of terracotta will also enhance your Mediterranean-style patio (see photo right) and go extremely well with Mediterranean plants.

Terracotta containers, a statue and wattle blooms may awaken memories of bygone holidays.

Scented surroundings

Many different aromas can be combined among leaf-scented plants like Pelargonium.

A Pelargonium flower.

Scents you can touch

Most leaf- or "contact"-scented plants (see How plants produce their scent, p. 8) originate from dry regions around the Mediterranean or from South Africa. Only by planting them in a convenient position can their full fragrance be appreciated, so they should always be within easy reach of a sitting corner where you can relax and gently rub a leaf between your fingers or stroke the tips of a scented bush. Place larger specimens alongside an access path where the aroma can be released when you brush past each plant. Plants like lemon verbena (*Aloysia triphylla*) or lemon-scented gum (*Eucalyptus citriodora*) are particularly suitable as both release an extremely intense fragrance at the slightest touch. The same effect can be triggered with lavender (*Lavandula*), catmint (*Nepeta*) and lemon balm (*Melissa officinalis*).

Aromatic leaves at different levels

Low-growing plants are very suitable for underplanting; make sure – as with all plant designs – that you only combine plants with similar care requirements in a container. *Plectranthus* and chamomile (*Anthemis nobilis*) therefore go well with angels' trumpet (*Brugmansia*).

Tall plants like scented geraniums (*Pelargonium*), clary sage (*Salvia sclarea*), bergamot (*Monarda*) or *Caryopteris* look better planted alone in large containers.

Plants with semi-erect shoots can be grown in hanging baskets. For example thyme (*Thymus*), low-growing mint (*Mentha*) and *Plectranthus* are excellent choices for such containers. Leaf-scented plants are generally more effective when arranged in small groups. Low-growing plants should be about knee high, for example on small plinths or iron plant ladders where they are able to

obtain sufficient sunlight to develop their full aroma. There they will also be at the right height to be touched. A box of different leaf-scented plants fitted to a balcony railing can be just as interesting as a strawberry pot filled with different species of thyme (see Strawberry pot photo, p. 10).

There are no limits to ideas for design. The danger of mixing together too many different fragrances is much less acute for leaf-scented plants, which release their aroma only when touched, than for flower-scented plants, which do not need an external stimulant to trigger their perfume. It depends entirely on which type of scent you wish to enjoy.

Multi-scented *Pelargonium*

Traditionally *Pelargonium* were standard balcony plants, but over the years they have been transformed into sought-after collector's items because of their willingness to produce flowers and their wide range of colours, shapes and scents. Much in demand are new, small varieties as well as the wild and scented species of *Pelargonium*, the common name for which is geranium. Scented *Pelargonium* nearly

all derive from wild forms or their hybrids (*P. graveolens*, *P. crispum*, *P. x fragrans*, *P. radens*). Their great variety of scents as well as their interestingly shaped and variously marked leaves will make up for their often-inconspicuous flowers.

Our tip: Several *Pelargonium* with the same or similar scents can be planted in a container, where they will rapidly intermingle to create a huge, scented "bush".

Different scents: From pineapple to cinnamon, the range of different *Pelargonium* fragrances appears almost inexhaustible as long as new hybrids are constantly being created. There are:

● Fruity aromas like lemon (*P.* 'Citronella', *P.* 'Mabel Grey'), orange (*P.* 'Prince of Orange'), apple (*P. odoratissimum* 'Variegatum'), pineapple, apricot, coconut and peach.

● Flowery perfumes like rose (*P.* 'Attar of Roses').

● Spicy odours like mint (*P.* 'Charity', *P.* 'Chocolate Tomentosum'), nutmeg (*P. x fragrans*), cinnamon, ginger and pepper.

● Resinous scents like cedar, elderberry and pine (*P.* 'Old Spice', which exudes a mixed pine-and-apple fragrance).

For yet more scents contact a *Pelargonium* specialist.

Scented surroundings

Year-round scent

The main season for fragrant flowers on balconies and patios is summertime, although late- or permanent-flowering plants can be enjoyed right into the autumn. A well-designed balcony or patio need not, however, look boring during the remaining seasons. Introduce a few evergreens with interesting, aromatic foliage and you will still be able to enjoy your little scented paradise even during the flowerless times of year. Evergreen plants that can remain outside during the winter are usually herbs like cotton lavender (*Santolina*) or lavender (*Lavandula*).

All-seasons plants

You can have an attractive flower box all year round if you choose evergreen dwarf conifers like cypress (*Cupressus*) as a permanent planting. They should not be spaced too closely together, however, so that, depending on the season, you can insert flower-scented plants like daffodil (*Narcissus*), sweet violet (*Viola odorata*), lily-of-the-valley (*Convallaria majalis*), *Phlox* or stocks (*Matthiola*) between the permanent plants. Evergreens will liven up your balcony or patio even in late autumn and through the long winter months into spring.

Colourful autumn magic

From early to mid-autumn, the last spate of flowers will bring yet another splash of colour to your patio or balcony. In a sunny, warm position close to the house, scented geraniums (*Pelargonium*), bergamot (*Monarda*), *Perovskia* and numerous herbs and spicy plants in pots will tirelessly produce their wonderful aromas until late autumn. To prevent the last remnants of scents from being dispersed by the wind, plants like angels' trumpets (*Brugmansia*), scented everlasting pea (*Lathyrus*), marvel of Peru (*Mirabilis jalapa*), *Phlox* and scented roses (*Rosa*) will reveal their fragrances only in a sheltered position. *Caryopteris* may not even start flowering until autumn, while some other plants may display certain interesting aspects of their character only in autumn. These memorable features may include some of the following.
Coloured foliage: Some, like *Trachelospermum* and Chilean jasmine (*Mandevilla laxa*), will also attract attention with their varied colour of foliage.
Berries: Others will not only entice birds with their eye-catching berries but will also provide pleasure for us humans with their brilliant colours. Particularly appealing berries appear on various species of honeysuckle (*Lonicera*) and the different species of *Viburnum*. Lily-of-the-valley (*Convallaria majalis*) also shows off its many bright red berries.
Caution: Honeysuckle, *Viburnum* and lily-of-the-valley are all toxic. As the attractive berries may well encourage young children to taste them, it might be better to make do without these plants if you have young children.
Autumn is not just a time for brilliant colours but is also a busy time for the gardener. The scents for spring need to be prepared now. Herbaceous and woody plants as well as bulbs and tubers of scented daffodils (*Narcissus*), lilies (*Lilium*) and hyacinths (*Hyacinthus*) require potting and placing in a frost-free position. Also start cutting back, moving and overwintering frost tender plants (see Pruning, p. 52, Overwintering, p. 54).
Our tip: When aromatic herbs are overwintered in a bright, cool position in the home, they should remain vigorous enough for you to pick their leaves occasionally for use in cooking.

Heady-scented heliotropes look superb in this planting of contrasting shades of lilac and yellow.

Care &
maintenance

Splendid flowering plants that also spoil
you with their enchanting scents require
a little bit of plant care if they are to
flourish. Provided you stick to the main
rules of care and overwintering, you
should be able to enjoy your plants for
many years.

*Top: Bergamot (Monarda) is one of the lesser-
known herbs.*
*Left: Proper care will ensure your scented oasis
flourishes on a balcony or patio.*

Care & maintenance

Careful plant selection

When choosing a plant, consider the plant itself and whether you can offer it the right conditions. Will the position you envisage suit it? Do you have sufficient space and the right conditions to overwinter large container plants? Also check the following points when buying.

● The general health of the plant. Ensure that it is strong and looks well cared for.

● The shape of the plant, which should be well balanced, with no bent or broken branches and twigs.

● The compost, which should be free of weeds and fungal infections. It should not be too firm nor wet.

● The rootstock, which should have plenty of well-developed roots. The roots themselves should look white.

● The leaves, which should be green, and any young shoots, which should be a paler green. Make sure that there is no damage to the leaves or evidence of pests.

Watering is vital

The right position is of course one of the most important prerequisites for a plant to flourish, but if a plant is not given the correct amount of water on a regular basis it will soon come to grief. Also important are when it is watered and how (see Watering, p. 50) and that the right type of water is used.

Many plants cannot cope with water that contains lime (hard water). You can contact your local water company to find out about the hardness of the water supply in your area. Water with less than 75 mg per litre (mg/l) of calcium carbonate is soft; 76–150 mg/l is moderately hard; 151–300 mg/l is hard; and everything above 300 mg/l is very hard, that means very alkaline or containing much lime. Only soft water is absolutely safe for all plants. Moderately hard water needs to be left standing for a while, and if your water is hard or very hard, you should only use water softeners or rainwater.

A colourful combination of fragrant plants.

Plant nourishment

It is much more stressful for a plant to grow in a container than in the open ground, where it can freely develop into the relatively unrestricted space of a bed or even in a completely uncultivated area. A pot-grown plant has its roots confined to a very small space, where there is minimal potting compost. The natural absorption of nourishment is upset and this therefore has to be supplied artificially in the form of water and fertilizer.

An abundant supply of fertilizer does not necessarily mean that a plant will flower particularly profusely or produce intense scent; in many plants, too much fertilizer may cause actual damage such as falling leaves, root damage and even the death of the plant. An overfertilized plant may well be impossible to rescue.

The correct level of fertilizer depends on the:
● Requirements of the species of plant.
● Growth phase of the plant.
● Type, nutrient content and concentration of the fertilizer.
● Fertilizer content of the proprietary potting compost, as this usually has already been enriched with fertilizer.

The type and concentration of the fertilizer depend on the nutrients required for the plant's relevant growth or flowering phase. The NPK values are indicated on the packaging (N stands for nitrogen, P for phosphorous and K for potassium) and these should be checked. Plants usually cope best with a balanced fertilizer.

Organic or inorganic fertilizer?

Because there is only a small amount of compost in a pot and a short growing season (mid-spring to mid-autumn), inorganic fertilizer is usually better suited to plants in large containers.

Inorganic fertilizer (artificial fertilizer) is immediately accessible for plants.

Organic fertilizer is created from animal or vegetable waste products like manure, blood, horn or bonemeal. These products are broken down and released through the action of micro-organisms in the potting compost so that they can then be absorbed by the plant. Depending on the amount of compost, the temperature and the available micro-organisms, it can take quite a while for the nutrients to become available to a plant that is fed with organic fertilizer.

Our tip: Fruit-bearing plants like *Citrus* and *Eriobotrya* absorb a general fertilizer well.

Herbs and spice plants, however, need a fertilizer containing very little nitrogen so that the aroma and flavour will not suffer from too vigorous leafy growth.

More fertilizer hints and tips

● Use a concentration of fertilizer corresponding to the manufacturer's directions to prevent an excess.
● Avoid using cheap fertilizer because it will often lack important trace elements; this could lead to the plant suffering from insufficient nutrients.
● Fertilize herbs and spicy plants only lightly as fertilizer may reduce the aroma.
● Never sprinkle fertilizer on plants with dry roots; it may damage them.
● Never allow the compost to dry out on plants that have been well fertilized.
● Plants should not be fertilized at all for two weeks after being potted into fresh proprietary potting compost; the compost will already contain fertilizer.
● Stop fertilizing large container plants by the end of late summer as fertilizer encourages the production of soft, new growth; all shoots need to ripen (mature) before the winter.

Watering plants

In addition to the use of the correct potting compost and fertilizer, regular watering is another important requirement so that plants can flourish. When positioned on a balcony or patio, however, container-grown plants are subjected to additional stress. Factors like sunlight, wind and rain will also influence their daily requirement of water.

Water quantities

By studying your plants over a long time, you will discover how much water each needs. You can also find out the rough water requirements of individual species in the plant portraits (see pp. 18–33) and in the table (see Scent calendar, pp. 34–5). As well as the special needs of individual species there are, however, some basic rules on when plants require water.

You need to water plants less:
● In cool or rainy weather.
● In shady positions or those sheltered from the wind.
● If growing in large containers that are partially sunk into the ground.
● If growing in plastic containers.
● During the resting period of the plant: this is usually in winter.
● At the beginning of the vegetative period: this is generally early to mid-spring.
You need to water plants more frequently:
● During the main growing season: from about late spring to early autumn.
● When it is very hot and there is little rain.
● In very sunny and windy positions.
● If growing in pots that are too small.
● If the plant has lots of roots.
● If growing in clay pots.
● If growing in poor-quality compost.

● If the plant needs large amounts of water and fertilizer (*Datura, Eucalyptus* and nearly all Solanaceae).

Correct watering techniques
Illustrations 1–3

Although watering by hand may be tedious and difficult, it should, nevertheless, be adopted as it is the correct method. Only in this way can the differing needs of individual plants be more easily catered for. *When watering with a watering can,* a stream that is too vigorous or constant on the same spot may create holes in the compost and uncover some of the roots.

1 A fine rose distributes water evenly.

2 A bath: first aid for a dried-out rootball.

When watering with a sprinkler attachment such as a rose (see illustration 1) the force of the water stream can be regulated. By using a watering lance (see illustration 3), the water can be more easily distributed into difficult areas.
Submerging the plant in a bath of water (see illustration 2) is good for plants with
● Very dense foliage.
● Dried-out compost.
● Root systems that are dense.
Here the rootball should remain submerged until no more bubbles can be observed rising up to the water's surface. Then allow the plant to stand where excess water can drain away.

Waterlogging is the greatest danger for all plants. This can be avoided by ensuring there is good drainage through the potting compost and out of the container. A thin layer of crocks, pebbles or Hortag on the container bottom can be separated from the compost by a piece of interlining fabric. This will not only allow the excess water to drain away but will also prevent rapid root growth through the drainage layer.

Drainage holes in the bottom of the container should be checked occasionally, as they can easily become blocked up with soil or roots, which will lead to waterlogging. Remove excess water at once from dishes under pots, particularly after heavy rain.

Permanent irrigation
Illustrations 4 and 5

Although watering by hand is definitely the best method of watering plants, you may need to use other methods if you are likely to be absent for several days. If possible, entrust the watering to a friend or neighbour with experience. You may, however, need to use one of the not very expensive yet reliable automatic irrigation systems that are now available.

Flower boxes with a built-in reservoir (see illustration 4) have a small amount of water in a double floor from which the plants can help themselves.

Clay cones (see illustration 5) are inserted in the compost and supplied by a water tank placed above the plants.

5 A raised tank and clay cones are useful if you are unable to look after your plants for a few days.

Useful watering tips

● Water in the morning or evening; this will give the plant the best chance of absorbing the liquid.
● Consider the influence of the weather. Check the moisture content of the compost. If necessary, remove the rootball from the pot.
● Use only hand warm water. Water that is too cold or too alkaline will harm many plants.

● Plants growing in inaccessible areas can be reached with a watering lance (see illustration 3).
● Fill the pot to the rim with water. Repeat several times, especially if the compost is very close to the rim.

● Water thoroughly, but do not waterlog.
● Avoid wetting the leaves and flowers as this can cause ugly leaf or lime spots.
● Give the plants definite rest periods when they are not watered much or at all.
● Do not use water that has previously been used for cleaning or bathing. Cleaning agents, bath salts or similar may damage plants.
● It is better to water too little than too much.

3 A watering lance for inaccessible containers.

4 A balcony box with built-in water reservoir.

Care & maintenance

Pruning

Occasionally large container plants – especially very big ones – will need cutting back so that they do not become bare or lanky. The most important types of pruning cuts are cutting back and thinning (see illustration right). When pruning, you should consider a few basic rules:

● Always cut just above an outward-pointing bud, so new shoots will grow outwards.

● Ensure the cuts are smooth, so there is no unnecessary damage to the stem.

● Large cut surfaces can be coated with a wound sealant (obtainable from garden centres).

Repotting

The right time for repotting is in spring. Only young plants should be repotted later than this, and then only if they require larger pots because of their rapid growth. Repotting will also be necessary if:

● The compost in the container becomes matted with roots.

● The plant leaves are hanging down. This indicates that all the nutrients have leached out of the compost through watering. If a plant is to be repotted in its old container, the roots should be carefully trimmed a little and any damaged ones should be removed.

Pruning techniques

Cutting back: Remove the diseased, dying and dead wood and shorten over-vigorous shoots. This encourages the formation of new shoots and more compact growth. It is also particularly helpful for plants that tend to become lanky as they mature.

Thinning: Cut out the inward-growing shoots so that air and light can penetrate better into the centre of the plant and to prevent the plant from becoming bare in the centre. Deciduous plants nearly always need to be thinned at least once a year.

The right compost

Always use good-quality potting compost for container plants. Cheap products will soon become leached and will not convert fertilizer very well. *Herbs in pots* prefer well-drained compost with few nutrients. Gravel, coarse sand or Hortag will reduce the compost's fertility and make it more permeable. You can also buy special herb compost. *Large container plants* are usually less fussy about their growing medium. Good-quality compost – made more porous with sand if appropriate – will encourage them to flourish. *Roses* love nutrient-rich potting compost. Garden soil enriched with compost may also suit potted roses.

The delicious scent of wallflowers comes in glowing colours of red, orange and yellow.

The correct way to repot

● Do not water the plants beforehand, as dry compost will make repotting easier.

● Remove dead roots and roughen up matted rootballs.

● Fill the pot with a drainage layer, a piece of interlining fabric and fresh compost (see Waterlogging, p. 51).

● Carefully insert the plant to be repotted.

● Fill any gaps with compost, do not press down too hard so root formation is not hindered in any way.

● Top up the potting compost to within 1–2 cm ($^1/_2$–$^3/_4$ in) of the rim. The space is needed for watering.

● Water the plant a little and do not fertilize again until about 2 weeks later.

● Stand the plant in dappled shade until it has recovered from the "repotting shock".

Our tip: Place plants in plastic pots and then insert these into clay or terracotta pots. This will save on watering and will cut down on the weight during repotting, clearing out or moving indoors.

Overwintering

All plants, no matter whether they are fully hardy or more tender, have to be prepared for the winter.

Winter protection outside
Illustration 1 to 4

Frost and damp may quickly damage plants that are left outside in winter, so shelter them from rain to prevent waterlogging. To help plants survive the coldest periods, choose some of the following alternatives.

1 Protect against frost with rush matting.

Partially burying. If you own a garden you may be able to partially bury garden plants in the autumn, either with or without their container. Cover up the root area with dry foliage, manure or conifer branches. You can stand flat dishes in a flowerbed.
Covering up (see Illustration 1). Move the plants close to a house wall and cover them up during short periods of frost with an old blanket, cardboard or plastic sheeting (but allow air to circulate).
Provide a cover. Build a small frame out of roof battens, anchor it well and cover it over with bubble wrap; provide facilities for ventilation.
Wrap up (see illustrations 2 and 3). Stand the container in a larger box or carton and fill up the gaps with old newspapers, polystyrene or wood shavings (see illustration 2). If necessary, tie additional polystyrene

sheets (from a builder's merchant) or bubble wrap (see illustration 3) around the large container. Always stand a large container on a warm base, for example a piece of polystyrene sheeting. Potted roses are a special case (see illustration 3). Their stem and shoots should be protected against premature shoot formation by covering them with a hessian sacking or conifer branches. In the case of frost-sensitive climbing plants, poke the conifer branches between the shoots (see illustration 4).

2 Polystyrene keeps roots warm.

Winter care for hardy plants

On frost-free days, plants that have been covered up should be well aired and, if necessary, watered sparingly. Shading them will protect them from the winter sun. Tall plants should be tied to a stick or trellis as they may be broken by strong winds.

Winter care for more tender plants

Container plants that are not fully hardy make greater demands on their winter quarters,

3 A standard rose protected with hessian.

and their requirements should be considered when choosing plants. You can overwinter these plants in a:

- Cellar or entrance to a cellar.
- Loft or attic.
- Cool entrance hall or stairwell.
- Garage or shed.
- Greenhouse.
- Warm conservatory.

The winter quarters should be frost-free, easy to ventilate and as bright as possible. A heating system with a temperature control is just as useful as an additional source of light. Polystyrene tiles will be helpful to prevent the plants getting cold "feet".

4 Protect climbers with conifer branches.

Bringing large container plants inside
Illustration 5

Cut each plant back (see Pruning, p. 52) before moving it indoors so there is more storage space in its quarters, and diseases may be prevented. Unhealthy shoots, flowers and seed heads should be removed as should dead branches and twigs. Remove all foliage from deciduous plants so it does not fall off in the winter quarters. Dry and dead leaves should also be removed from the surface of the compost (see illustration 5).
Our tip: You can also remove any more diseased or dried leaves when you prune further in spring. Initially, bring in only frost tender plants, then move in the rest according to their degree of sensitivity.

Winter care
Illustration 5

As plants absorb only small amounts of

5 Sweep dead leaves from the soil surface.

6 Remove lanky shoots and faded leaves.

water during their rest period, the rootball should not be too wet when they are brought indoors.
Evergreen plants should be positioned near a window.
Deciduous plants should be placed in the dark.
Plants should be well spaced so air can circulate and there is

enough room left to reach the plants. The rule of thumb is: the cooler the place chosen for their winter quarters, the less water they will need. The rootball should be slightly damp.
The following checks should be made:
- The temperature and humidity daily.
- For pests weekly. At the same time remove lanky shoots and dead leaves (see illustration 6).

Our tip: Ventilate the winter quarters well on frost-free days.

Moving plants back outside in spring

More robust species can be taken outside again before the last cold snap in spring. Position them close to a house wall to protect them from late frosts. More tender plants should be moved outside once all danger of frost is over. Then prune each plant and repot. Initially water and feed sparingly until sufficient foliage has formed.

Care & maintenance

Pests & diseases

Healthy plants find it easier to resist pests or diseases as they are strong and vigorous. If an infestation does occur in spite of optimal care, you need not immediately reach for a killer spray. Try to offer your plants the best possible position and stick to these few rules of prevention.

Prevention rules

● Check the plants for infestation before buying them.
● Newly bought plants should not be mixed with other plants for 2 weeks.
● Check where a plant should be positioned as well as its watering and feeding needs.
● Keep plants well spaced. Depending on their position, ensure there is fresh air and sufficient humidity.
● Regularly remove dead leaves and flowers.
● Avoid cold water, watering too often, waterlogging and overfertilizing.
● Regularly check the plants for infestation and move sick specimens at once.
● Once a year, strengthen plants by dosing them with trace elements (available from the specialist trade).
● Use the gentler methods initially if infestation occurs.
● Get expert advice in good time before experimentation creates even more damage.
Caution: Wait for a few days before consuming any herbs or spice plants that have been treated with plant protection agents. The flavour and aroma of the plant may be affected.

Fast aid for sick plants

If an infestation occurs, you should always seek out the reason. This could be that pests have been "introduced" through purchased plants, watering has been incorrect, the compost may be waterlogged, the air too dry or too moist, or the plant may be in the wrong position. The sooner you recognize these care mistakes, the more likely you are to be successful with the more gentle methods of pest control. The following will provide fast help in controlling the most frequently occurring pests.
Aphids: Strip them off or spray them with a concentrated stream of water; spray with a liquid soap and spirit solution.
● Use 15 ml (1 tablespoon) each of liquid soap and spirit in 1 litre (1³/₄ pints) lukewarm water, and mix well.
Scale insects: Wash off with soap solution or spray down evergreen plants with needle-like leaves with meths.

Spider mites: Introduce beneficial predatory insects; change the position; increase the humidity.
Our tip: A "plant sauna" will drive away spider mites and increase any spray effect.
● Water the plant well, cover with a transparent plastic bag, make it airtight and leave to stand like that for a few days.
Whitefly: Stand the plant in the wind; introduce beneficial predatory insects or yellow tags; if infestation is severe, use an insecticide.
Grey mould: Space the plants further apart; keep them in a better ventilated position; do not use fungicide unless infestation is extremely severe.
Sooty mould: Wash the leaves with clear water.
Inexplicable symptoms of damage: Lack of light, water that is too cold or cold "feet", a draughty position, great fluctuations in temperature or humidity can all cause plant damage. These physiological disturbances reflect the way some plants react to the cold, regardless of whether it is caused by watering, draughts or cold "feet" and produce warped, curly or buckled leaves. For example, this can be seen in *Cassia corymbosa*. Once affected the leaves will not return to normal, although fortunately the plant won't be permanently damaged.

Angels' trumpet and tobacco plants do not release their aroma until after darkness falls.

Index

Authors' notes

This volume deals with designing with scented plants on balconies and patios as well as with their care. Some of the plants described are toxic. Lethal plants or even less toxic ones that may create considerable health problems in frail adults, children or domestic pets have been marked with a skull-and-crossed-bones symbol in the section on plant portraits (pp. 18–33) and in the table (pp. 34–5). Make absolutely sure that children and domestic pets do not eat the plants that have been designated as dangerous. Also ensure that pots, containers, boxes and hanging containers are firmly fixed.

When using plant protection agents, always follow the manufacturer's instructions on the packaging. Store plant protection agents and fertilizers (even organic ones) in a place that is inaccessible to children and domestic pets. Consumption of these agents may damage health. They should not be allowed to come into contact with your eyes. If you sustain an injury while handling soil or compost, visit your doctor to discuss the possibility of having a tetanus vaccination.

The meanings of the seasonal indicator abbreviations used on pp. 18–35 are as follows:

ESP = early spring
MSP = mid-spring
LSP = late spring
ES = early summer
MS = mid-summer
LS = late summer
EA = early autumn
MA = mid-autumn
LA = late autumn
EW = early winter
MW = mid-winter
LW = late winter

Photographic acknowledgements
Becker: p. 32 left, 33 right centre, 41, 47 right; Caspersen: p. 12; Eisenbeiss: p. 22 right; Gsanger: p. 23 bottom; Konig: p. 18 bottom, 20 bottom, 22 left, right, 37 right; Mein schöner Garten/Eigstler: p. 32 right; Mein schöner Garten/Kogel: p. 33 bottom left; Morell: p. 19 left, 24 top; Nickig: p. 3 left, 5 right, 10, 14–15, 21 left, 28 bottom, 33 right centre, 53, 64/inside back cover; Pforr: p. 24 bottom, 28 top, 33 top; Reinhardt: p. 19 right, 21 right, 26, 27 left, right, 36–7; Seidl: p. 23 top, 27 left; Reinhard: p. 23 top, 27 left; Silvestris/Brockhaus: p. 15 right; Silvestris/Voss: p. 18 top; Stork: 2, 3 right, 4–5, 7, 39, 42 top, bottom, 45, 46–7, 48, 57; Strauss: 9, 17, 20 top, 31; Transglobe Agency/ Caspersen: inside front cover.

Cover photography: L. Rose.

Acknowledgements
The authors and publishers would like to thank Dieter Stegmeier, of Essingen, for his expert advice on the subject of scented *Pelargonium*.

Cover photographs
Front cover: *Magnolia stellata; lavandula; gardenia; sweet violets.* Inside front cover: *A carpet of rose petals; a wonderful scented potpourri can be prepared from these.* Back cover: *'Peace' roses on a verandah.*

Reprinted 1999

This edition published 1998 by Merehurst Limited
Ferry House
51–57 Lacy Road
Putney
London SW15 1PR

© 1997 Gräfe und Unzer GmbH, Munich

ISBN 1 85391 679 X

Fnglish text copyright © Merehurst Limited 1998
Translated by Astrid Mick
Edited and typeset by Joanna Chisholm
Printed in Hong Kong by Wing King Tong.

Carnations – Decorative plants even in a pot

Roses, violets, lilies-of-the-valley, lilacs and carnations are probably the flowers that most people think about first of all in connection with scented flowers.

All these plants – as well as many less well-known species – can be grown in large containers on your balcony or patio. In the case of carnations (*Dianthus*), which are among the most beautiful of fragrant plants, you should plant the low-growing species. Larger species will not find enough space in a pot to remain erect so will tend to bend over. By choosing the right carnation species, you will, however, be able to enjoy this classic scented plant on your balcony or patio.

Carnations provide a splendid wealth of flowers that will last for several months in summer.